The Silence Between the Sighs

MIMI NOVIC

Aspiring Hope
Publishing

British Library Cataloguing Publication Data.
A catalogue record for this book is available from the
British Library

ISBN 978-0-9954539-0-6

published by Aspiring Hope Publishing

In the Name of God the Most Beneficent, the Most Merciful.

Only my Lord knows the secret of my ever longing heart,
And only you know who you are, who made the silence sing its song,
which took the loneliness away.
In gratitude, in hope, in humbleness, in Love.

ABOUT THE AUTHOR: Mimi Novic

$\mathcal{M}$imi works as a therapist, alternative medicine practitioner, life coach, writer, author and poet.

She teaches and runs workshops and seminars in holistic therapies, alternative medicine and self awareness and has worked around the world in clinics, retreats and on a one to one basis.

She has specialised and devised a breathing technique, called "Healing Breath Peaceful Soul" which is a method of deep meditation and awakening through the power of breath.

Her inspirational writing has now entered another chapter and has embarked upon the mystical journey of healing through music.

She has beautifully harmonised her inspirations with soul enlightening music through her inspiring adventure Aspiring Hope Music.

Each piece of music has been been especially composed to accompany her thought provoking and inspiring words, that awaken our heart to the beautiful universes within ourselves.

Through her various works people are able to experience the subtle nature of healing and awaken to themselves.

Mimi grew up in the English countryside, where she took her inspiration from the days and nights spent in the natural world that surrounded her, which taught her that everything in nature as well as with people has its own language and wants to be heard.

From early childhood she began to realise, that to spend time alone, in solitude and contemplation, we can be transported to a state of being where we can find the answers to life's questions and translate them into words and it is in this state of solitude that the heart alone can understand us.

It is in the moments of silence, that we can be taken to our own universe, where our real essence longs to be part of.

Through her work she encourages others to embark upon the most wonderful of quests and that is to find their reason for being on this earth, to remember who they are.

By encouraging ones heart to speak, it gives you an eternal door through which you can walk through, so you are able to find the true purpose of your existence.

By healing our past & our present ultimately gives us hope for the future of our dreams and aspirations.

Once we learn the beautiful language of love, we may understand the language of everyone's heart and thus find the key to Eternity.

FOREWORD

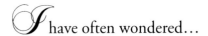I have often wondered…

What is to be born?
What is it to be given life?
What is it to give birth?
What is it to love?
What is it to give love?
What is it to receive love?
What is it to be love?
What is it to have compassion?
What is it to give compassion?
What is it to be compassion?
What is it to be in heaven?
What is it to be part of heaven?
What is it to glimpse heaven?
Where is heaven?
What is it to have hope?
What is it to give hope to others?
What is hope?
What is it to pray?
What is it to become part of someone's prayer?

What is it to be prayed for?
What is it to have your prayers answered?
What is it to have a friend?
What is it to be a friend?
What is it to find a friend?
What is it to keep a friend?
What is it to lose a friend?
What is it to have faith?
What is it to gain faith?
What is it to lose faith in yourself?
What is it to believe in yourself?
What is it not to believe in yourself?
What is it to dream?
What is it to lose your dreams?
What is it to yearn?
What is it to be yearned?
What is it like to be touched?
What is it to hold someone's hand?
What is it for someone to hold your hand?
What is it like what is it to have your dreams come true?
What is it to hold your friends hand?
What is it to let go of your friends hand?
What is it to remember your beloved's hand in yours?

What is it like to kiss?

What is it like to be kissed?

What is it like to want?

What is it like to be wanted?

What is it like to be born knowing that you left your beloved?

What is it to then search for your beloved your whole life?

What is it that you find that it was your beloved that was the one searching for you?

What is it to be lost?

What is it to lose?

What is it to find?

What is it to be found?

What is it to smell the fragrance of roses?

What is it to be the perfume?

What is it to live?

What is it to die?

What is it to be reborn?

What is it never to die?

What is it to find eternity?

What is it to glimpse eternity?

It is to be eternal…

What is it to see?

What is it to be seen?

What is it to be remembered?
What is it to fly?
What is it to soar beyond the hemispheres?
What is it like to catch a star?
What is it to glimpse the universe in the blink of an eye?
What is it to spin around the galaxy?
What is it to adore your face?
What is it to tremble at your beauty?
What is it to feel your breath upon my soul?
What is it to lay in the palm of your hand?
What is it to be caressed by your love?
What is it to be whispered your pleasure?
What is it whirl in ecstasy?
What is it to hear your voice?
What is it to obey your voice?
What is it to carry your light?
It is to be free to travel beyond time and space?
What is it to follow your heart?
It is to soar above the earth and follow the trail of stars.
What is it to be afraid of your dreams?
It is to stand still.
What is it to believe in your hearts voice?
It is to hear the voice of Angels.

What is it to sing?
What is it to hear a song?
What is it to dance?
What is it to be entwined with love?
What is it to be in love?
What is it to be loved?
What is it to have wings?
What is it to have wings and never know?
What is it to have wings and not know how to use them?
What is it to discover you have wings?
What is it to be afraid of your wings?
What is it to discover at the end of your life that you had wings
and never flew?
What is it to have a moment?
What is it to hold a moment?
What is it to be the moment?
What is it to lose a moment in your life?
What is it to find out that you were hidden from yourself?
What is it to be forgotten?
Each day we are forgotten by ourselves, through ourselves,
For we do not believe, in who we are.

I have placed my feet upon this earth, yet my soul is carrying me elsewhere.

I do not try to belong, for there is nowhere I would want to be.

I have tried to escape, yet, the body has its reasons, and the heart has its promise.

So I try, in humility, to continue upon the dusty road of the now and as I meet the souls who were destined to share a moment of heavens remembrance with me, I see that many pass me by and although some are looking, they are not seeing.

Some are seeing, yet they are lost, and some are holding their hearts in their eyes, hoping to be found.

My heart remembers…

Maybe, through these words upon the pages of your life,
you will remember also, that which you to promised.

*O*h ye who travel the world seeking that which is nearer to you than your own breath,

Look into your heart

Look into your heart

There lie the treasures you seek.

This life is but a doorstep to heaven.

Sometimes, with just a glance, a moment can be captured, That is imprinted on your heart forever.

May your steps of courage and faith,
always lead you to the path closest to God.

It is through faith that we find peace.
And above all,
It is in loving that we find life.

$\mathcal{T}$ime and distance mean nothing to the ones whose hearts have been woven by the golden thread of friendship.

We may walk in the past with our memories,
Never with our footsteps.

For the tide to join the seas,
It must first take a step forward, and surrender.

We are but shadows upon the water
Nothing more, nothing less.
Reflections of the mirror of the Divine
Existing in this world, but only for a moment.
Then in a blink of an eye, we are gone,
Gone forever.

The only guarantee is the Eternal.
The Absolute, who
guides those whom He
wills, when He wills,
for always.

*W*hat is it to lose a friend?

It is to lose a part of your hearts memory of the past.
The footsteps of sorrow walk upon the heartache, while the dust
rises and with it caresses the eyes, so they shed their tears of
sadness.

The soul yearns, but the heart knows that within this world,
time is but an instant, and then it is gone and all things,
including the ties of friendship are temporary, unless bound by
the thread of the Eternal weaver whose hand sews destiny.

Our existence is temporary upon the waves of time,
We are but shadows among the mists of memories.
All we can be we must be in this moment,
or we disappear instantaneously.

Only the perfume of our memory lingers amongst
the dewdrops of time.

A place where only a few have knowledge of
A time where only a few have found themselves in
This land is visited by only those who completely believe in the
deepest depths, of the caverns of their hearts;
The voice that is calling them.
To reach this place of suspended beauty, within this lifetime,
One must accept themselves, unconditionally.
For then, one can free their souls and fly from the chains of
this world.

It is in making the journey, that we are able to arrive.
It is in leaving, that we may find our destination.
It is in our fears, that we may find courage.
It is in our weaknesses, that we may find strength.
It is in believing, that we may find our dreams.
It is in laughter, that we may find contentment.
It is in caring, that we find others.
It is through prayer, that we find God.
It is in trusting, that we find hope.
It is through our tears, that we find compassion.
It is in acceptance of ourselves, that we gain life.

We walk into this world unknowing the length
of the journey that we have embarked upon.

We only know that we must complete it.

What lies ahead remains unseen,
What lies behind disappears
All that remains is the way.

It is up to us how we travel upon it.

$\mathscr{I}$ have travelled the waves of the biggest oceans.
I have felt the crest of the highest wave beckon me.

How can I ever look back, and merely stare at the puddles and find joy?

I still recall the smell of sea air
I still hear the echoes of the oceans breath
I still feel the grains of sand between my footsteps
I still walk this journey in solitude, yet never alone.

How can I be the blade of grass in the winnowing winds,
Upon the dunes of the loneliest deserts, so empty to the eyes of man.
How can one be in such silence, that angels dare not to murmur?
As long as one is with his Lord, then all of creation is holding its breath.

How can one ever truly be?
By renouncing himself.
By renouncing all that he ever thought, all he ever was, all he
ever could be.
Renounce all, oh travellers upon this road to love
For nothing is yours and nothing ever will be.
Renounce your life as you think you see it
And become life, as He wills it.

Lose yourself in Him, and there you shall be found.

From the mountain tops of the highest peaks, to the music of the winds breath, to the silence of the soul.
Who is it that whispers to me my hearts wishes each moment? Who is it that with every living breath renders His wish for me?

The yearning He alone placed in me, He longs also to fulfill through me, for He alone created, with His Divine, ever living, ever creating life force, all that can be and all that ever will be, all that ever was.

Who alone placed this ravaging fire of yearning to be all that You want me to be, so that I may adore You, know You, as You want to be known.

For You create, destroy, give birth, re-create, as only You alone know how, as only You alone can, for You are the creator, who creates with each new moment a new beginning, an ending, a re-birth.

Wanting to be known, calling us back to ourselves, calling us back to You, so we may admire, adore, cherish, glorify at the most intimate levels of the throne; the seat of all existence

The seat of all creation, the throne of all.

Each one of us, Your creation who You moulded with Your own hands, You placed a thousand and more journeys, so we may reach You, ultimately.

You placed a different longing, a different desire in each of us, for each one has a quality, a sphere of light from Your existence within us, representing a part of Your magnificent being, Your never ending existence. Glory be to You.

We are part of You, Your magnificent, glorious, existence.

Each atom within me glorifying the never ending One.

Running, whirling, spinning, dancing, living, yearning to meet with You.

Yet You are within me, You are all of me how else could I exist?

How else can anything exist or be without You? Never.

My heart and soul entwining with the beloved, how can I be separate from my lover?

To be separate means to die, but we are eternal, never ending, or beginning, forever....an eternity and more.

You placed within me the desire of the beloved, because he is part of You.

He reminds me of You, he is the unity of life within my essence.

It is Your breath that You placed upon my soul, the murmur of His heartbeat that I await, for then, we are as one.

The form of the physical, a manifestation of the Divine in the visible world.

When the spiritual and physical worlds merge into one, a new life is created, for when the worlds join in the promised union of the heart, soul and body, an explosion of Divinity rains upon the kingdom of heaven and within the celestial galaxies, continues to spin through the universes of creation.

For two beings to be submerged within this unison, their love is bound by the atoms, the heartbeats melting upon the sparks of existence, their souls expanding, joining, surrendering to each other in humbleness, in hope, in prayer, in yearning, that eternity's breath, breathes infinity into them.

*O*h Truth! Oh Manifest One! O Ever living One!

For You alone we await in the darkest nights of the soul, In the glorious days of the spirit.

Oh Ye who are everything and are everywhere, we are asking to be for You and You alone.

We are these created beings, moulded by the Hand who creates all and then breathes His breath into all.

Oh our, Lord, You are our all. You alone we yearn to be with, with no one else.
And nothing else, for You placed these yearnings within us from the promises of Your breath.

We feel the trembling upon the soul each time You remind us of Your promises, for You alone keep Your promises.

Each one of us knows our purpose, and the way in which You ask to be glorified.
Oh how we know our purpose, oh how we know.

You have shown us the beauty of our existence.
Shower upon us Your grace so that we may be enlightened, so that we may be guided, so that we may answer to Your voice.

We have always known the secret.

We have always known the truth.

But we hide it from ourselves through ourselves

Each and every one of us arrives at the place within us, the
gateway to the door of heaven, at the destined hour.
There we see the reality of who we are.

How can we ever claim to own anything,
when only He is the creator?

We did not create ourselves; it is He who created us.
Therefore it is an illusion, and everything that we think we are,
we are not.

Everything we thought we were, are going to be, we are not.
Everything we think we own, have owned, want to own,
we cannot.

This imagination that we are so powerful is but a mirage on the oasis of existence.

Our complete power, our complete existence, is coming from the Creator.

If we believe in the positive, we are in tune with our Lord, for He is the ultimate positive.

If we are negative, and keep dwelling in the pit of negative thoughts, and actions, then we are clasped in the clutches of our ego,

For our ego wants to be king, but this can never be.

The key to the doors of paradise are held by the remembrance of our secret; that we carry the throne of our Lord within the abundance of our heart.

Here abides the one and only truth.

The touch, the sparkle, the moment, the entwining, the beauty of the stillness of the longest day.

When you blow Your breath beneath my wings, then I must fly into the worlds, parallel to the earth, beyond the earth, high above into the hidden realms, as far and beyond the earth as forever is.

The flight of the spirit is like no other. For the spirit moves according to its masters command.
The energy that is summoned is enough to illuminate a thousand and one worlds.

Light must move, must penetrate, must alight, enlighten inside the souls, the hearts, and fly in between heartbeats, it cannot be contained. Therefore it must be used.

When there is a surge within us such as this, we must give it to the master, who may carry it.

It merges, it expands, and then there are explosions of fragments of stars. Who is aware may bathe, those that deny, disappear in the process.

We can only be free if we are accepting, that in every second that transpires, in every atom of the moment, change occurs, re-born are the fragments of time.

Therefore we are constantly moving, spinning around the source in constant motion, we are never still, yet there are moments of stillness, moments of silence, yet silence moves, it moves us to another dimension of being.

If we are silent, we are in the music of the Divine orchestra.

There are times when our spirits power is so strong that only the entwining of His will can shape the energy of the Divine within.

To be touched by someone in this state of being, is to be touched by the Divine hand.

We are but vessels of the celestial, running through us, gushing forth from the springs of the eternal One.

We are only what He made us, nothing more.
His glory runs through us, for He is the substance from which our fountains of life flow.

Around, around, above all of creation He guides us. He created our souls with the wings of flight, our bodies with the taste of earth.
We must accept that only in the merging of the two are we complete.

We are all incomplete until the explosion of the heart's desire carries us to a place suspended above all, the place where he places us upon His breast, and whispers:"Now you are home".

*W*e stand looking at the mirror of ourselves and do not recognise the eyes filled with tears that hide the oceans of separation.

We search for the winds of destiny, yet they are the breath that we breathe.

We look for the limitless horizons that carry us towards forever, yet the vista of forgetfulness falls like dust upon us making us forget who we are.

We stand on the bridge of yesterday and the fountains of our past empty themselves into the reflections of the forgotten dreams we once dreamt as children and the light of our hopes begin to fade.

We do not awaken, until the shadows fall upon the valley of sorrow and we are stirred only by the crumbling of the walls that we have built around our hearts and we ask the ever unanswered question;
Where did our life go and to whom did we give it to?

*O*h our Lord!

How does one glorify You to encompass all Your glory?
By sacrificing the world?
By sacrificing the body?

Oh how foolish we are.
What is the world; it is not ours to give up.
What is the body? Yours and Yours alone, for the One who
creates, must own that which He makes with his own hands.

Oh by love, Oh by love, we must try.

The truth of love's droplets raining from paradise gardens,
encapsulated in a moment when the breath is murmuring
upon the souls bed of flowers, Divine drops, within each one a
universe of existence holds its breath for its creation to unfold.

And in a flash of the Divine spark, a life is created, then it is
given a form, a shape, so it may glorify in the tongues of the
celestine beings, for its entire existence.

Oh our Majestic One, when did You begin to tell us of the story of our creation?
You sang it to us from the moment You shaped the clay, watered the form, and You spoke "Be", and it was.

You created us because You wanted to be known.
Oh our Creator, Oh our destination, oh our life!

We search for You everywhere, yet You are here.
You are where You always were, it is us who separate ourselves from You through our ego.

There can be no separation, there is no me and You, there is only You, in everything, in everyone.
All is One nothing else exists.

And all of creations are but fragments floating upon the eternal pool of existence.

Oh people oh creation of all the worlds of existence, jump into the pool of reality, of surrender, where you will lose everything, but gain all.

The ultimate surrender is that of falsehood and illusions, of which all, is but dust, upon the mirror.

As long as we are grasped by the wants of the ego, we shall never be free. When we surrender to the song of the Beloveds wish, we are the wings of the bird of life, flying upon the endless horizons, amongst the rainbows of the limitless dawns within us.

The Desert asked the Meadow:
"How do you survive with all these flowers around you?
 Do they not over crowd your spirit?"

"Aah" replied the Meadow
"Don't you know, it is because of them that I have a spirit."

And the Meadow asked the Desert:
 "How do you survive, being so alone?"

"Aah "replied the Desert
"It is in being alone, that I survive."

The beauty that awaits you,
The peace that inspires you,
The happiness that beckons you,
Do not push it to one side
Do not deny that it is there.

Each morning with the suns rising, bathe in its rays.
Each day with the brightest light,
Surrender to its beauty.
Grow in its opportunities,
Accept the dream that you are dreaming,
Listen to its voice,
Hear the song your soul is singing.

Since this is the reality within,
Make the steps towards hope.
Step into your happiness
Follow your heart today.

With a glimpse of sorrow within my eyes,

I wept at moments that were lost, because I was afraid.

Afraid that I would never be re united with you.

Years flew by on the breeze of my sighs,

Until I caught the sight of your face.

The ocean within my soul blew a wind across the sky,

And my reflection of being, I glimpsed, upon the flight of your spirit.

It beckoned me to join the winds of change, to let go of the sorrow, to grasp your hand and to be taken to where courage takes flight and gives wings to the brave.

The place of unparalleled equilibrium of the axis within the pendulum which swings past time that resides within the rooms of your ever tender heart,

Whose gates are opened with the caress of love's whisper upon your heart.

The circle of existence knows no beginning and no end. What people assume to be heaven after this worldly existence is in fact something we live through within each moment.

There is no death.
And there is no life.
There is only the abundance of the Supreme, eternal magnificence.

We only know we are, because the One reflects with His mirror.
How else would we know, would we see ourselves?
We look, and yet we see nothing.
We listen, but we hear not a murmur.
We talk, yet we say nothing.

We are just an illusion of the senses of the physical world. For in this material world, we are in non existence;

We are as fragments of a memory, dancing within a single raindrop that falls through the hands of angels, as they sparkle amongst the stars upon the starlit heavens, appearing, and then disappearing.

Yet our light remains forever, glistening, among the sweetly fragranced petals of paradise.

*W*e travel upon this road but once, and we leave our footprints with each step we make in this life.

Although we may glance back at the moments we have shared with one another, and cry tears of joy or of regret,
We can never re trace the times we missed to tell one another how much we cared.
How much we were moved by their very presence in our lives.

We do not always have the courage to speak the words of the heart, for the fear of the disapproval of others.
We do not always have the strength to stand up for what we believe, for the fear that others will extinguish our truth.

But with gentleness, with sincerity, with faith in ourselves,
We can always be true, true to ourselves
True to the souls that matter.

The ones who carry the torch of loves light deep in their hearts,
Who will be our companions, our friends, the rare few, who
will share our journey, for a few years or more.

Those that can teach us, that when we look to now,
We can find peace within this moment, just by believing.

So my friend, when you glance back at the footprints that you
have left behind,
May you look upon them, always, as steps to your happiness.

As the wind whispers, the heart wonders, where did all those unexplained moments go?

For so many years we feel like our life is a preparation for the ultimate realization, yet our life is the realization.

Then suddenly the gates of destiny fly open, and we find Ourselves unable to resist the urge to fulfill all that we promised Him.

With His help, with His grace, we are unable to hold back this wind within us, the holy breath yearning to move within us, through us, to move according to the Divine hand, where between His fingers, the rivers of paradise flow and water the magnificence of His creation.

The birth, the death, the re-birth, all is one. For separateness does not exist.

The harmony of the Divine symphony resonates within all of us, within all of the beauty that echoes its music, as the sound of each heartbeat pulsates according to the master.

We are all but unsung symphonies, waiting each moment for the sign to sing that song that our soul yearns to harmonise in words.
Our life is but the Lord's promise to us, that He will take us home.
Therefore, where is our existence?

Our life is the proof that we search for constantly, that we have a purpose.
We are, the proof that God exists.
We are the treasure that we are searching for.

*W*hat does the heart possess the most?

Surely it is the loneliness of the separation of the Beloved's touch upon its tender breast.

Caressing the separation, so it becomes familiar, to prepare for the gift of life.

*Y*esterday, was a place we visited only once in our life.

Tomorrow is somewhere where we may never place our footsteps.

Yet today, we have a moment in our hands that we can capture and make it last beyond the hands of time,
Touching upon the everlasting splendour of forever.

*W*here do the hands of infinity clasp each others fingertips of time?

Where do the hands of saints and mystics touch the glory of eternity?

Where can we kiss the lips of those that have spoken the words of truth?

Where can we meet love?

Tell me, oh tell me, oh sweet bird of paradise, you that whispers the dawn, that hears the lament of the heart at the midnight hour.

Whisper to me where are the answers to the questions I seek?

"Oh, oh, oh, how pitiful your cry is oh creature of God.

Stand in front of the mirror of yourself; look into the eyes that see you,

Open your ears to the sound that beckons you speak to the One who is listening, what answers do you search for?

You are the answer!"

Fragments of memories of where our bare feet
tread upon the pebbles of time,
Slowly being washed by our tears of missed opportunities,
Yet somehow, could we have done anything differently?

Eventually no matter how far you walk,
No matter how many teardrops fall,
No matter how long the journey,
You arrive.

Because in order for a journey to have a beginning,
You must first place your feet upon the infinite moment.

As the echoes of yesterday, resonate within our heart,
Our life journey unfolds before us.
As the memories fade,
The only one thing that remains, is those that we love.

*O*nce, when lying in the ruins of pain and suffering,

When no one could see the horizon within my eyes,
And all about me fell to ashes,
When no one understood the sorrow of my tears,
Love came and took me by the hand...
And led me to the desert of despair that covered my soul.

I saw the loneliness and sadness through my tears, as each one dropped, so full of regrets and longing for mercy to rain upon my heart.
Then in an instant before me, lay the carpet of existence.

Love gently lay me down and caressed me with the Divine winds, whose touch was so gentle and so beautiful.
It whispered so quietly, that only those rare heartbeats could hear its voice. "Did you think that I had forgotten you?"
And slowly it continued to speak to me its pearls of infinity.

"The desert of ourselves, is a barren and empty place without the company of love.

Take my hand once more, come and surrender to me, so that all that was in ruins can be re built.

So that all your pain, I can caress and heal.

So that all the tears that have flowed, I will wipe away.

And be sure, that despair will never accompany you again.

My only request, and nothing more I ask of you,

Is that you give to me yourself.

And in turn, I shall give to you life.

This is my eternal promise".

From the moments of silence in childhood dreams,
To the loneliness of never belonging,
Remember the distant winds whispers:
"You are the secret that you seek,
You are the silence of peace after a thousand sighs,
And the loneliness of never belonging,
Is the echo of your memory, as you left your footprints in the hearts of those you loved".

$\mathcal{S}$ome people wait a lifetime for a moment to be touched by love.
Some die never having felt it.

How do we recognize the moment when it alights upon our life?

Close your eyes, Close your eyes,
And surrender, surrender,
Until the wings of your heart embrace your spirit and you ask for nothing more than to fly towards the edge of existence.
Then and only then will you know the essence of love.

We go to sleep each night wondering if it is our last.
We wake up each morning and wonder where our days
have passed.

Sometimes we hear the distant echo, the music of our heart.
Sometimes we hear the heartbeats wondering how long they
will last.

To hear our heartbeat, surely means that we are alive?
Yet how many of us that are alive, are actually living?

No one can lift you, if you don't want to stretch out your hand?
your hand?
Who can take you anywhere, if you don't want to go?
Who can stand by you, if you want to be alone?
Who can enter your heart if you don't open the door.

At the breaking of the dawn,
The thread of the new horizon beckons:
"Come forward"
The heart sings:
"Take me towards my dreams let me awaken with the melody of hope within my ears,
And the song of joy upon my eyes".

One day it's going to be too late,
When you wish you had said
what was in your heart,
And the moment left, and with
 it took your friend.

What is moving, us or now?

Now cannot move or it ceases to be.

It has nowhere to go.

We, in perpetual motion of pre eternity towards eternity, are moving and existing in between reality and now.

Our true existence is glorifying the One whom we stand in front of and gaze upon His infinite face without a beginning or end.

Our reality is in front of Him, that what we see here on earth and in the realms of the physical and non physical are a single ray of His light that shines through our manifestation on earth and the hidden worlds.

The creations that we see with the eyes of the tangible worlds are just reflections of the truth.

We are all truth.

The journey is to unveil the heart of the hidden realities and become free of the senses.

We are always in the now or in the reality, all else is an illusion.

Our very essence of realization is that we are in existence because He exists, we do not appear in the worlds, only as mere fragments of the sublime do we travel in and amongst the celestial universes that rotate around the axis of time.

To which there is no time, it is endless, as it showers the rains of heaven upon the creations of infinity.

$\mathcal{E}$very day our heart is beating, asking to be recognized by someone who will allow it to be free to sing its desires.

Every day, even without realizing, we are wasting moments upon moments, afraid to move according to our deepest inspirations.

Every day, we miss the chances that life presents us to be with those that touch our hands in a way that could make us fly.

Every day, something inside us dies, because we do not have the courage to follow our dreams.

Every moment, every hour, every day, every year,
And the sands of time pour themselves into the seas of yesterday, into oblivion, where we can only recognize our life by standing, looking into the mirror of our tears.
This is all we have as a glimpse into who we are, who we were,
And yet, as we close our eyes to wipe away the tears, even the glimmer we had is lost,
And the memory of ourselves disappears.

We stand looking at the mirror of ourselves and do not recognise the eyes filled with tears that hide the oceans of separation.

We search for the winds of destiny, yet they are the breath that we breathe.

We look for the limitless horizons that carry us towards forever, yet the vista of forgetfulness falls like dust upon us making us forget who we are.

We stand on the bridge of yesterday and the fountains of our past empty themselves into the reflections of the forgotten dreams we once dreamt as children and the light of our hopes begin to fade.

We do not awaken, until the shadows fall upon the valley of sorrow and we are stirred only by the crumbling of the walls that we have built around our hearts and we ask the ever unanswered question;
Where did our life go and to whom did we give it to?

$\mathcal{M}$y life I hold in between moments of joy and happiness,
Yet the happiness I found along the way emptied into
nothingness. What was weaved amongst the silence of sadness,
the tears of regret, was the longing of my Beloved.

As the hallmark of longing was etched upon my heart, bliss
took me by the strings of the harp of my soul and began to
play the music of forever.
Contained, were a thousand unsung pieces of unheard
melodies of the ever encircling, still seas of never ending
existence.

As the tears of unfulfilment dropped into the ocean of longing,
as the sands of lost memories began to fall, each descent carried
with it countless cries of the soul's yearning to be nothing, so
that from nothing it can join into everything.

Disappearing momentarily, losing all existence.

As nothingness it became, it exploded amongst the universes of celestial gatherings.

As the lights of the paradise sunrises gathered, into each explosion of the reality,
A never ceasing, never-ending, sublime power showered its beauty of whispering droplets of waterfalls of serenity upon my being,
There was my Beloved, in the ceasing, to be.

Where does the deep sense of stillness within ones soul begin to urge the ripples of the ever expanding heart, to keep pursuing its moment of expansion, when it seems that the horizon of truth overshadows all fears of abandonment?

Where can we find that everlasting peacefulness that echoes towards the never-ending dawns of destiny, that urge us to keep flying through the tiny grains of dust called time?

Can we ever hold the times that we lost within the grasp of our hands?

Never.

We must gently move in between each passing footstep of yesterday and today and dance towards tomorrow.

Yet we miss the moment to dance upon the flutter of the passing now,
And then we wonder, where did our life go, into which river of the passing yesterday did we sit and wait by the shoreline, for someone to call our name?

By the time we hear the call, it is too late,
For time has emptied its moments.

From the flutter of the birds wings,
To the murmur of the sigh of a new born child,
To the constricting of the soul, awaiting to be born,
Wanting the journey to begin, yet feeling sorrow at leaving their Beloved.

For to be born, means for the soul to be caged, imprisoned, for a few years or more.
Yet the yearning to be free, is but a glimpse of an instant when we shall be beyond the prison of the body,
A time when the soul will soar as a bird drunken in ecstasy, wanting to be free as it flies towards the hand that awaits its long awaited arrival, from the journey through the life of separation,
Waiting to caress its sorrowful song, as it is welcomed home once again.

The thread of all creation,

The life, the meaning,

The reason, the completion,

The beginning with no beginning, where everything became, and all that it was, all that it ever will be,

Where is it oh travellers of this road that has only one destination?

The silken thread of life, that is the masterpiece of existence, is woven with the breath that you breathe.

It came into being, before you.

It moved the heart, before you.

Yet there is no sound, its stirring can only be heard through the melody of silence that gently blows its breeze before you came to be.

Find this solitude amongst the crowds of creation,

And you will find yourself.

No one knows when the gates of the heart will fly open.

Sometimes, we can sit a whole lifetime outside the gates of our own heart, held prisoners by our fears, our regrets, our unfulfilled hopes, We can even be held prisoners by others actions, that lead us to many deep and sorrowful nights.

When it seemed that the rising of the dawn, was far enough never to shine its light upon our face.
Our heart contains the essence of our life.
Our soul wants to follow the secret of its desires.
Yet we are the ones who stop ourselves through ourselves.

The lifelong question that lies upon everyone's lips, that beats in every heartbeat, that whispers in moments of deepest silence:
"Where is the river that we can be watered with hope?
Where are the oceans of love that may bathe the eyes that have wept, Heal the hearts that have been broken,
And give new life to the hearts that thought they had died?"

When you are in the circle of Divine manifestation,
When the wheels of destiny spin inside the roads that lead to
the fields that contain the flowers of yesterday,
The perfume of yearning sprinkles the dust of remembrance of
the Beloved's embrace upon the breast of tenderness.

As the memory entwines within the pathways of long forgotten
times,
The flicker of light that remains is upon the brow that sheds
the drops of suffering at the separation of life's dawn, that
contain never ending dewdrops waiting to be born into the
morning breeze, that blows its promised winds upon the lips of
the lover,
Becoming the breath that speaks,
Only to those that can hear the footsteps of angels,
As they leave their ever gentle footprints on the heart.

Sometimes we don't know why we meet the people we do, until they leave our lives.

Sometimes we share our life with people and yet never really know them or ever truly meet them.

Yet sometimes we may be with someone for only moments of our life and feel as if we have known them a lifetime.

Their arrival in our lives shows us what was missing within ourselves.
Their departure leaves only a deep sense of loss and we know no one else can ever fill the emptiness.

We spend too much time with those that never touch our heart, ignite our spirit, or make us feel alive, yet those that we love, we hardly see and our encounters with them last less than the glimpse of a tear drop.

The soul penetrates the worlds and the realms, as the particles of light disperse around the universes, collecting the energies of the frequencies, which make them spin faster as they gather momentum.

God wanted to be known and therefore created all creation to be known.
The only reason for our existence is for Him to be known.

He, out of pure love created the crown of creation, the beloved of the Lord,
And for him He created everything, so that we would love him.
He is the vessel of love, where we pour our love lights drop by drop, and he carries them to our Lord.
So if we are created for the sake of the beloved, the most beautiful, the shining moon among moons,
Our sole purpose is to follow his example, to please him, to support him.
His creed, his existence, is alive in everyone and everything.
The holy souls never die.

These elevated, sublime, beautiful, Divine beings,
Whom our Lord invested His power and glory,
Came to earth and blessed the earth and all the worlds and universes.
Their presence lives forever.

They are the love springs, our nectar that pours forward in droplets in oceans upon our souls, our bodies, our universes endless blessings,
Lights upon the very essence of our being.
These enlightened ones, are the universes, spinning, ever flowing, never ceasing to shower upon us the heavenly rains, that give us support, life, movement towards our destiny.

Each has a universe, a world, a galaxy,
And with each breath of surrender, we are able to disperse our soul in such a way that it is penetrating the ever beating, ever living heart of the Lord,
The most glorious, the all merciful, the all powerful,
The only One.

When we were created, we were in awe at the splendour of the face who created us.

We gaze upon it, within it, around it, yet in it.

Do you think we ever stopped looking?

Do you think we ever left our Beloved?

Never, Never, Never.

It can never be, because our reality is glorifying the Beloved.

What we are here on earth, in the worlds and hidden realms, is but a ray or two.

A part of us left the Divine presence, because we were given the chance to show ourselves in the worlds through His emanating love.

We continue, in love.

There are lands and worlds and universes beyond us and within us, unexplained places that beckon us with each new breath that we inhale and exhale.

It is in between these two breaths that we think of as nothing, rests our life, as if suspended for the glimmer of a moment, here abides the secret beyond all secrets.

Who has ever believed in the stillness of the moment?

How can anything ever be still when it is in constant ebb and flow towards the final destination.

Our breaths are waves of yearning to be with the most beautiful, most sublime, Almighty Lord of all heavens and earth, of the created worlds, the uncreated worlds, the majestic and only One king who reigns over His creation, calling back to His infinite ocean the waves of our tremors of the fearful heart to surrender to His call, to surrender to His embrace, to join the sea of truth.

Oh how it must be to be beckoned in every stirring of the soul.

We are the dreams of our Lord.

He is the reality; we are the dreams that exist only
because of Him.
Yet we do not exist, He is the only One in existence.
Where are we?
Where do we belong?
Where did we come from?
To where are we going?

From nothing, into nothingness.

The love of my life has left and taken me beyond myself. No one can find me only those that loved me enough to stop searching.

It seems that so many moments have passed through the winds of time, unexplained ripples of the heart, where eternity seemed to hold its breath.

How I miss the tenderness of the touch of a thousand nights that last a lifetime…Only an essence of Divinity could grace my very existence in this world and the others with the never ending yearning of love and all its endless sighs of separation from my Beloved.

Oh Beloved, oh my life, oh my purpose for being, for breathing, for yearning in the depths of the darkest nights and the dawns awakening lament, I call for You and You alone.

I call in hope, in tears, in amazement, in awe of Your face, beckoning for a glimmer of light for the spectacular beauty of Your glory to embrace me, to hold me, to caress me.

And then there is you, who lifted me to the angel's choir and gave me a reason to live.

For when the beauty of their Divinity swept past the ears of my heart, they sang the book of my life in such grace of being, that the unbearable lightness of being embraced the promise of everlasting eternity and I took the hand of fate and accepted the promise that I made to You.

For my purpose they sang and encouraged this heart of mine to beat again.

With the promise that each heartbeat would be in praise of You, in hope of You, in expectance of You, in the depths of the pulsating soul the heart would transmit its message for all those asleep to awaken to the calling of their Lords invitation:

"Come, Come, Come, remember Me, for I remember you,
With each breath you take, I am calling you back to Me, leave everything,
And in an instant, you may be with Me."

One day you will wake up and find that your friend has slipped away.

Neither a word nor a murmur they left behind,
Only their memory in your tears

In the land of dreams, I walk with you.
In sadness, I will comfort you.
In happiness, I will rejoice with you.
In life, I will take you by the hand and dance with you.
In my heart, I carry you.

Sometimes all we need to soothe our soul and ease our burdens,
Is the loving hand of a friend gently touching our heart,
And lifting us towards love.

With a tear in my eye,
With a song in my heart,
I thank God everyday for putting me on the path next to you.
How beautiful it makes the journey of life.

$\mathcal{E}$very day we wonder
how we enter the secret world where are dreams are,
the place of peace, beauty, love.

The lock lies in our hands,
the key, in the heart of a friend.

As the hands of time sweep past the minutes of our life,
As I begin to walk the path towards you,
I hear the echo of a song.
If your heartbeats whisper my name,
Leave the door to your heart ajar.

I remember the days we used to walk hand in hand,
When time stood still to let us dance.
Then came the call that calls everyone,
and took your hand out of mine,
And a part of me died.

Our whole life we are amongst many, yet we walk in loneliness.

We walk with people, yet we feel alone.

Only when love takes us by the hand, will it never let us go.

How many moments are written for us,
With whom will we spend them?

How long is this road,
To where is it taking us?

Is there anyone yearning us,
How long will they wait?

Who are we missing,
Do they remember us?

Where we got lost,
Will anyone find us?

In whose heart is written our name?

*L*oneliness, my friend that accompanied me all my life.
Happiness, sometimes held my hand.
Pain, kept me humble.
Stillness, gave me understanding.
Tears, gave me compassion.
Suffering, made me pray.
God gave me hope.
Faith, kept me walking.
My dreams, gave me courage.
Fear, kept me prisoner.
Love, set me free.

It is not the touch that matters, it's whose hand caresses us.
It is not the glance that matters, it's whose eyes are seeing us.
It is not who hurt us that matters, it is who heals us.
It is not the pain that matters, it's who takes it away.
It is not who lets us down that matters, it is who picks us up.
It is not who lets us go that matters, but who we want to go with.
It is not whether we live that matters, but whether we feel alive.
It is not where we are that matters, but who we are with.
It is not what people say about us, that make us who we are.
It is not possible for others to keep us prisoners, if we want to be free.

The world will be left without you one day,
But inside you now there is a world still waiting to be born.

The internal struggle of the believer of love penetrates the boundaries of every heart.

The outward form of the person, resonates the frequency of the mysterious and powerful force of the Divine within all of us.

When we meet again in this world, we are re connecting with each other's souls and fulfilling the promise we made in the unseen world, where we once met and made a promise in front of the Infinite One.

One day you will wish that you could hear the sound of their voice,
Smell the perfume of their memory,
Feel the gentleness of their touch,
Put your hand in theirs,
Feel the warmth of their smile upon your heart.
But time came and took them away and then we realised that we were too late to tell them;
"Oh how we loved them".

I have stood at the gates of loneliness,
And I walk through them each day.
I have sat down with regret,
And it taught me how to seek forgiveness.
I have gazed upon the distant stars,
And they showed me the way home.
I have made friends with pain,
For it showed me how to pray.
Tears came and washed away the sadness,
And I asked them to stay.
Then one night, love came and offered me its hand,
And I have never it go.
We may walk in loneliness,
We may know sadness,
We may feel pain and we may weep,
But the heart whispers with each sigh:
"Keep my door open, so that I to, may hold the hand of
love again

One night as the fragrant perfume of yesterday, lingered between the thread of tomorrow,

The window of solitude flew open, and the bird of destiny, spread its wings.

As the wind of change swept past the fragments of time, unlived moments, unsung melodies, unspoken secrets, waited for the Heavenly rain to shower its splendour,

So that destiny could write, with the ink of Love, my name amongst the stars,

So that one day, someone while looking to the glorious skies, would remember, for a fleeting second,

That there once was a soul, who once lived,

And now was no more,

*O*h my sweet beloved…Hush my darling please don't cry,
Know that one day we all must die.
Know that when our final day will come,
Our job on earth has been done.
Take my hand and hear my song,
Know that one day soon it won't be long,
Before the tears begin to say,
I wish I'd had one more day
To hold you close beside my side.
I wish I could have sung your praises far and wide.
But I know I left it for far too late,
As the heavens finally opened their gate.
Know my love that I miss you,
Know my love as you lay asleep,
Know that when you hear the whisper of the wind,
I will sing to you my lullaby.
Know that this is not goodbye,
But as angel's ears hear my prayer,
And in my heart I will you keep you there.
When you hear the flutter of their wings,
Know it is then that my soul finally sings.

Lightning Source UK Ltd.
Milton Keynes UK
UKOW02f1936261116
288618UK00001B/2/P